MW00985902

RZIM Critical Questions Discussion Guides

# Is God
# Real?

## William Lane Craig
## & Charles Taliaferro

**SERIES EDITOR** Ravi Zacharias
**GENERAL EDITOR** Danielle DuRant

Inter-Varsity Press
Nottingham, England

IVP Connect
An imprint of InterVarsity Press
Downers Grove, Illinois

InterVarsity Press
P.O. Box 1400, Downers Grove, IL 60515-1426
World Wide Web: www.ivpress.com
Email: email@ivpress.com

Inter-Varsity Press, England
Norton Street, Nottingham NG7 3HR, England
Website: www.ivpbooks.com
Email: ivp@ivpbooks.com

Published in association with the literary agency of Wolgemuth & Associates, Inc., Orlando, Florida.

InterVarsity Press® is the book-publishing division of InterVarsity Christian Fellowship/USA®, a student movement active on campus at hundreds of universities, colleges and schools of nursing in the United States of America, and a member movement of the International Fellowship of Evangelical Students. For information about local and regional activities, write Public Relations Dept., InterVarsity Christian Fellowship/USA, 6400 Schroeder Rd., P.O. Box 7895, Madison, WI 53707-7895, or visit the IVCF website at <www.intervarsity.org>.

Inter-Varsity Press, England, is closely linked with the Universities and Colleges Christian Fellowship, a student movement connecting Christian Unions in universities and colleges throughout Great Britain, and a member movement of the International Fellowship of Evangelical Students. Website: www.uccf.org.uk.

Adapted from William Lane Craig, God, Are You There? (Norcross, Ga.: RZIM, 1999) and Charles Taliaferro, Does the Idea of God Make Sense? (Norcross, Ga.: RZIM, 2002).

Design: Cindy Kiple
Images: David Buffington/Getty Images

USA ISBN 978-0-8308-3151-7
UK ISBN 978-1-87784-222-6

Printed in the United States of America ∞

| P | 19 | 18 | 17 | 16 | 15 | 14 | 13 | 12 | 11 | 10 | 9 | 8 | 7 | 6 | 5 | 4 |
|---|----|----|----|----|----|----|----|----|----|----|---|---|---|---|---|---|
| Y | 23 | 22 | 21 | 20 | 19 | 18 | 17 | 16 | 15 | 14 | | | | | | |

# Contents

# Introduction

I was at an airport looking for my departure gate, and I noticed that the flight listed was to another city. So I asked a passenger if that flight was headed to Atlanta or elsewhere. She promptly answered my question and told me the notation was wrong. As I thanked her and turned to find a seat, she said, "Are you Ravi Zacharias?" I answered yes. Then came this utterly surprising response: "I listen to you on the radio regularly. I didn't know you had questions as well." I laughed at her compliment and assured her that I had several questions, especially if I want to get to the right destination.

There are so many answers out there and a question to every answer. To ask them is to engage with information. To ask questions about life's ultimate questions is to be in the pursuit of God. That's what this series is about: to take you to the heart and mind of God, which is the right destination.

In this series, critical questions raised by thinking minds are answered by those who have asked them themselves, and found the answer in the person and teaching of Jesus Christ. There are writers in this series that I have heavily leaned on myself. They are trained in the art of critical thinking not merely for the intellectual stimulation it brings but for the ultimate pursuit: the bridge between the heart and the mind so that thinking shapes being, which in turn impels doing.

In our time such helps as this series are invaluable. On every side, be it the academy or the movies, just enough doubt is cast on the person of Jesus that minds are left unsteadied in their trust in the Scriptures and the truth claims of the gospel. Such doubts and questions are rarely answered by a one-blow argument. Life is not as simple as that. In fact, any worldview that depends on one such knockout argument flirts with logical and experiential extinction.

Life closes in on us from multiple sides. That is why a good apologetic starts with the fundamentals before it deals with the specifics. From the nature of truth to the incarnation of it in Jesus, from the trustworthiness of the Scriptures to the questions of moral reasoning, they are addressed here. These succinct and interactive discussion guides will stir your mind and occupy a much-used section in your library.

I sincerely hope this series will be both a tool of equipment and a source of inspiration. Darrell Bock in his study *Can I Trust the Bible?* sums up the content of these slender volumes well:

> If there is the possibility that God has spoken through this text and has participated in the history it records, then the answers to our questions are not a mere academic exercise. Our journey back into these seemingly foreign, ancient times may be a real opportunity to see more clearly who we are and were created to be.

A couple of words of appreciation are well in order. First, the original effort in putting this all together was done by Paul Copan. In this instance, the hard work as general editor is by Danielle DuRant, who labored long to make this accessible. I am also grateful to InterVarsity Press for seeing the value in this short series and taking the step to publish it. Those of us who study this material will be the beneficiaries.

Questions will haunt as long as the mind is alive. The answers of Christ will inspire and instruct because he is the author of life.

*Ravi Zacharias*

# Getting the Most Out of This Guide

William Lane Craig begins his booklet *God, Are You There?* (Norcross, Ga.: RZIM, 1999) with this pointed question: "Is there a personal, transcendent being who created the universe and is the source of moral goodness?" Charles Taliaferro, in *Does the Idea of God Make Sense?* (Norcross, Ga.: RZIM, 2002), recognizes "*another* motive for investigating the idea of God: what if it turns out to be more than a mere idea?"

Craig and Taliaferro contend that how our universe came to be and how we may account for right and wrong (objective moral values) are best explained by the existence of God. Furthermore, they show that although we intuitively know that objective moral values are undeniable, if God does not exist, then neither do they.

In this discussion guide we will examine a number of reasons why we can confidently believe that God exists and, moreover, that he is knowable. The Scriptures tell us that the one who seeks God earnestly will find him. This promise will be our guide in the pages and questions to follow.

## ■ SUGGESTIONS FOR INDIVIDUAL STUDY

1. As you begin each session, pray that God will speak to you through his Word.

2. Read the introduction to the session and respond to the opening

reflection question or exercise. This is designed to help you focus on God and on the theme of the session.

**3.** Each session considers a particular passage or passages of Scripture, and is supplemented by the author's commentary. Read and reread the text before engaging the questions.

**4.** Write your answers to the questions in the spaces provided or in a personal journal. Writing can bring clarity and deeper understanding of yourself and of God's Word.

**5.** It might be good to have a Bible dictionary handy. Use it to look up any unfamiliar words, names or places.

## ■ SUGGESTIONS FOR MEMBERS OF A GROUP STUDY

**1.** Come to the study prepared. Follow the suggestions for individual study mentioned above. You will find that careful preparation will greatly enrich your time spent in group discussion.

**2.** Be willing to participate in the discussion. The leader of your group will not be lecturing. Instead, he or she will be encouraging the members of the group to discuss what they have learned. The leader will be asking the questions that are found in this guide.

**3.** Stick to the topic being discussed. Your answers should be based on the texts provided and not on outside authorities such as commentaries or speakers. Only rarely should you refer to other portions of the Bible. This allows for everyone to participate in in-depth study on equal ground.

**4.** Be sensitive to the other members of the group. Listen attentively when they describe what they have learned. You may be surprised by their insights! Each question assumes a variety of answers. Many questions do not have "right" answers, particularly questions that aim at meaning or application. Instead the questions push us to explore the topic more thoroughly. When possible, link what you say to the comments of others. Also, be affirming whenever you can. This will encourage some of the more hesitant members of the group to participate.

5. Be careful not to dominate the discussion. We are sometimes so eager to express our thoughts that we leave too little opportunity for others to respond. By all means participate! But allow others to also.

6. Expect God to teach you through the material being discussed and through the other members of the group. Pray that you will have an enjoyable and profitable time together, but also that as a result of the study you will find ways that you can take action individually and/or as a group.

7. Remember that anything said in the group is considered confidential and should not be discussed outside the group unless specific permission is given to do so.

8. If you are the group leader, you will find additional suggestions at the back of the guide.

# 1 Who or What Made God?

The very idea of God itself is perhaps the most significant idea in human thought and culture. Even if there is no God, the very idea of God merits sustained inquiry.

Yet there is *another* motive for investigating the idea of God: What if it turns out to be more than a mere idea?

## ■ OPEN

What or who was your earliest introduction to God?
How have your ideas about God changed over the years?

## ■ STUDY

Some of the lines of Handel's *Messiah* have their origin in Isaiah 40, which opens with "Comfort, comfort my people, says your God." The prophet Isaiah reminds his audience that God is all-powerful, all-knowing and eternal, to whom no one else can compare. We read in this chapter of God's promise of deliverance and restoration for the people of Israel suffering under exile and enslavement in Babylon. *Read Isaiah 40:12-14.*

<sup>12</sup>*Who has measured the waters in the hollow of his hand,*
    *or with the breadth of his hand marked off the heavens?*

*Who has held the dust of the earth in a basket,*
*or weighed the mountains on the scales*
*and the hills in a balance?*
[13]*Who has understood the mind of the LORD,*
*or instructed him as his counselor?*
[14]*Whom did the LORD consult to enlighten him,*
*and who taught him the right way?*
*Who was it that taught him knowledge*
*or showed him the path of understanding?*

**1.** In a few phrases, how would you describe the God Isaiah introduces in this passage?

**2.** Note that Isaiah poses rhetorical questions five times in these three verses. How do these questions encourage you to consider who God is?

**3.** How does the prophet see God active in the world?

What difference would it make if you sensed that this eternal God was active in your own life?

Let's consider the following mainstream theistic conviction: There is no deity or being or force or law of nature that brought about or explains why God exists. Moreover, this lack of cause or external explanation covers not just the very being of God but God's fundamental properties: the divine attributes of being all-knowing, all-powerful, omnipresent and good. Judaism, Christianity and Islam are united in upholding the idea that God's very being is not dependent on any cosmic or worldly powers.

The lack of external cause is not an embarrassing oversight, as if theologians painted themselves into a corner without planning a means of escape. In fact, the belief that God—as the ultimate, supremely great being—requires no external cause is the basic contribution of monotheistic traditions to the philosophy of God. While you and I—and this cosmos as a whole—may require external causes to exist, God enjoys a different footing. God is the ultimate foundation for all other reality.

**4.** Reflect on the sidebar. If God did not create himself and God's very being is not dependent on any cosmic or worldly powers, what can you conclude about God's existence?

**5.** Why might theists be accused of painting themselves into a corner regarding an explanation for God's existence?

*Read Isaiah 40:18-28.*

[18]*To whom, then, will you compare God?*
*What image will you compare him to?*

¹⁹As for an idol, a craftsman casts it,
    and a goldsmith overlays it with gold
    and fashions silver chains for it.
²⁰A man too poor to present such an offering
    selects wood that will not rot.
    He looks for a skilled craftsman
    to set up an idol that will not topple.
²¹Do you not know?
    Have you not heard?
    Has it not been told you from the beginning?
    Have you not understood since the earth was founded?
²²He sits enthroned above the circle of the earth,
    and its people are like grasshoppers.
    He stretches out the heavens like a canopy,
    and spreads them out like a tent to live in.
²³He brings princes to naught
    and reduces the rulers of this world to nothing.
²⁴No sooner are they planted,
        no sooner are they sown,
        no sooner do they take root in the ground,
    than he blows on them and they wither,
        and a whirlwind sweeps them away like chaff.
²⁵"To whom will you compare me?
    Or who is my equal?" says the Holy One.
²⁶Lift your eyes and look to the heavens:
    Who created all these?
    He who brings out the starry host one by one,
        and calls them each by name.
    Because of his great power and mighty strength,
        not one of them is missing.

[27]*Why do you say, O Jacob,*
    *and complain, O Israel,*
  *"My way is hidden from the* LORD*;*
    *my cause is disregarded by my God"?*
[28]*Do you not know?*
    *Have you not heard?*
  *The* LORD *is the everlasting God,*
    *the Creator of the ends of the earth.*
  *He will not grow tired or weary,*
    *and his understanding no one can fathom.*

**6.** Compare verse 18 with 25, and verse 21 with 28. Describe the effect of these questions on you as a reader.

**7.** How is God superior to the rest of creation?

How do the writer's words here align with your own understanding of who God is?

**8.** Isaiah reminds his audience that God is not only both King and Creator but also that he personally cares for all that he has created (verses 26-28). To what extent might this knowledge change your understanding of the world and your relationships?

Maybe everything we observe *does* have an origin; we can imagine the origin and demise of our planet, solar system and galaxy. But this does not so much mean that there is no God or that it is likely there is no God as much as it means that these things in the cosmos are not themselves God. It is the *contingency of the cosmos* and the things around us that can lead us to think there is a God who made the cosmos. In fact, the universe's absolute origin has been ably substantiated by astrophysicists and cosmologists. If contingent object A is explained by B which is explained by C and so on into infinity, we will never get a complete or fully satisfactory explanation of A. Where did you get this booklet? If you borrowed it from A who borrowed it from B *ad infinitum*, we would fail to achieve an adequate explanation of your possessing the booklet now. By locating the cause of the cosmos in a self-existent or necessary being, God, we recognize a being that did not borrow its existence from something else.

**9.** Based on the reading, explain how the contingency of the world (its dependence on something else to exist or to be sustained) logically leads to belief in the existence of God.

**10.** "These things in the cosmos are not themselves God." What are some examples of how people treat created things as though they were God? (See, for instance, verses 19 and 20 above.)

How should a correct understanding of God's uniqueness affect how we treat such things?

## ■ GOING FURTHER

Write out your thoughts and questions about God's existence. You might want to spend some time reading through Isaiah 40 as well as Psalm 8. In the coming days and weeks, consider adding more thoughts or revising what you have written.

### Additional Reading

For an abbreviated but thoughtful discussion of the question of God's existence, read pages 189-94 of Ravi Zacharias's *Can Man Live Without God?* (Dallas: Word, 1994).

# 2 | Does God Make Sense of the Universe?

GENESIS 1

Have you ever asked yourself where the universe came from or why everything exists instead of just nothing? Typically atheists have said that the universe is just eternal, and that's all. But surely this is unreasonable. Just think about it a minute. If the universe never had a beginning, that means that the number of past events in the history of the universe is infinite. But mathematicians recognize that the idea of an actually infinite number of things leads to self-contradictions. For example, what is infinity minus infinity?

## ■ OPEN

What reasons would you give for why the world and life exists? Or, to put it another way, why does life exist rather than nothing at all?

## ■ STUDY

Jews and Christians attribute the book of Genesis, as well as the next four books of Scripture, to Moses' authorship and compilation. These five books comprise the Pentateuch ("five volumes"), some of the oldest material in the Bible. The first chapter of Genesis takes us back to the beginning of the universe; yet unlike a dry textbook, it unveils the Creator's handiwork through highly stylized poetry and narration. **Read Genesis 1:1-25.**

[1]*In the beginning God created the heavens and the earth.* [2]*Now the earth was formless and empty, darkness was over the surface of the deep, and the Spirit of God was hovering over the waters.* [3]*And God said, "Let there be light," and there was light.* [4]*God saw that the light was good, and He separated the light from the darkness.* [5]*God called the light "day," and the darkness he called "night." And there was evening, and there was morning—the first day.*

[6]*And God said, "Let there be an expanse between the waters to separate water from water."* [7]*So God made the expanse and separated the water under the expanse from the water above it. And it was so.* [8]*God called the expanse "sky." And there was evening, and there was morning—the second day.*

[9]*And God said, "Let the water under the sky be gathered to one place, and let dry ground appear." And it was so.* [10]*God called the dry ground "land," and the gathered waters he called "seas." And God saw that it was good.* [11]*Then God said, "Let the land produce vegetation: seed-bearing plants and trees on the land that bear fruit with seed in it, according to their various kinds." And it was so.* [12]*The land produced vegetation: plants bearing seed according to their kinds and trees bearing fruit with seed in it according to their kinds. And God saw that it was good.* [13]*And there was evening, and there was morning—the third day.*

[14]*And God said, "Let there be lights in the expanse of the sky to separate the day from the night, and let them serve as signs to mark seasons and days and years,* [15]*and let them be lights in the expanse of the sky to give light on the earth." And it was so.* [16]*God made two great lights—the greater light to govern the day and the lesser light to gov-*

ern the night. He also made the stars. [17]God set them in the expanse of the sky to give light on the earth, [18] to govern the day and the night, and to separate light from darkness. And God saw that it was good. [19]And there was evening, and there was morning—the fourth day.

[20]And God said, "Let the water teem with living creatures, and let birds fly above the earth across the expanse of the sky." [21]So God created the great creatures of the sea and every living and moving thing with which the water teems, according to their kinds, and every winged bird according to its kind. And God saw that it was good. [22]God blessed them and said, "Be fruitful and increase in number and fill the water in the seas, and let the birds increase on the earth." [23]And there was evening, and there was morning—the fifth day.

[24]And God said, "Let the land produce living creatures according to their kinds: livestock, creatures that move along the ground, and wild animals, each according to its kind." And it was so. [25]God made the wild animals according to their kinds, the livestock according to their kinds, and all the creatures that move along the ground according to their kinds. And God saw that it was good.

**1.** What is the first description of the earth that we are given in verse 2?

What surprises you about this description?

**2.** What do you make of the phrase "the Spirit of God was hovering over the waters"? What does this tell you about God and his relationship to the world?

**3.** The writer repeats the phrase "God saw that it was good" in verses 10, 12, 18, 21 and 25. What does this commentary say about our world?

The contemporary atheist philosopher Kai Nielsen gives this illustration: "Suppose you suddenly hear a loud bang . . . and you ask me, 'What made that bang?' and I reply, 'Nothing, it just happened.' You would not accept that. In fact you would find my reply quite unintelligible." So why does the universe exist instead of just nothing? Where did it come from? There must have been a cause which brought the universe into being. As the great scientist Sir Arthur Eddington said, "The beginning seems to present insuperable difficulties unless we agree to look on it as frankly supernatural."

We can summarize our argument thus far as follows:
1. Whatever begins to exist has a cause.
2. The universe began to exist.
3. Therefore, the universe has a cause.

Given the truth of the two premises, the conclusion necessarily follows.

Now from the very nature of the case, as the cause of space and time, this supernatural cause must be an uncaused, changeless, timeless and immaterial being which created the universe. It must be uncaused because we've seen that there

> cannot be an infinite regress of causes. It must be timeless
> and therefore changeless—at least without the universe—be-
> cause it created time. Because it also created space, it must
> transcend space as well and therefore be immaterial, not
> physical.
>
> Moreover, I would argue, it must also be personal. For how
> else could a timeless cause give rise to a temporal effect like
> the universe?

**4.** According to the excerpt above, why must the cause of the
universe be supernatural?

**5.** This cause must not only be supernatural but also *personal*.
What could lead to this conclusion? Would you agree or dis-
agree? Why or why not?

.

### Read Genesis 1:26-31.

*26Then God said, "Let us make man in our image, in our likeness, and
let them rule over the fish of the sea and the birds of the air, over the
livestock, over all the earth, and over all the creatures that move along
the ground."*

*27So God created man in his own image, in the image of God he cre-
ated him; male and female he created them.*

*28God blessed them and said to them, "Be fruitful and increase in
number; fill the earth and subdue it. Rule over the fish of the sea and the
birds of the air and over every living creature that moves on the ground."*

*29Then God said, "I give you every seed-bearing plant on the face of the whole earth and every tree that has fruit with seed in it. They will be yours for food. ³⁰And to all the beasts of the earth and all the birds of the air and all the creatures that move on the ground—everything that has the breath of life in it—I give every green plant for food." And it was so.*

*³¹God saw all that he had made, and it was very good. And there was evening, and there was morning—the sixth day.*

**6.** What does the phrase "Let us make man in our image, in our likeness" (verse 26) reveal about God? What does it reveal about our intrinsic value and worth?

**7.** Verse 27 is a poem (and the first occurrence of poetry in the Old Testament). Why are so many terms repeated in this passage? How does the last stanza of verse 27 ("male and female he created them") fit with the rest of the poem?

**8.** Compare the refrain in verses 10, 12, 18, 21 and 25 with the one in verse 31. What does this tell us about God's view of all of his creation?

What might the inclusion of this unique phrase after the cre-

ation and blessing of human beings tell us about our position
in God's eyes?

> Scientists once believed that whatever the initial conditions
> of the universe, eventually intelligent life might evolve. But
> we now know that our existence is balanced on a knife's
> edge. It seems vastly more probable that a life-*prohibiting*
> universe rather than a life-*permitting* universe like ours
> should exist. The existence of intelligent life depends upon
> a conspiracy of initial conditions, which must be fine-tuned
> to a degree that is literally incomprehensible and incalcula-
> ble. For example, Stephen Hawking has estimated that if the
> rate of the universe's expansion one second after the Big Bang
> had been smaller by even one part in a hundred thousand
> million million, the universe would have re-collapsed into a
> hot fireball. There are around fifty such quantities and con-
> stants present in the big bang, which must be fine-tuned in
> this way if the universe is to permit life. And it's not just each
> quantity, which must be exquisitely fine-tuned; their ratios
> to one another must be also fine-tuned. So improbability is
> added to improbability to improbability until our minds are
> reeling in incomprehensible numbers.

**9.** Describe how the initial conditions for the beginning of the
universe make sense of a Creator God.

**10.** What does the universe's complexity and delicate balance reveal about us as human beings?

**11.** How might the idea of a God who created you in his image shape your understanding of your purpose and identity?

### ■ GOING FURTHER

Take time to journal or talk with someone further about this study, perhaps giving thought to what it means to be made in God's image.

### Additional Reading

Ravi Zacharias observes that every worldview must answer four questions: origin, meaning, destiny, morality. For a response to this first question, see Zacharias's chapter "Is There Not a Cause?" in his book *The Real Face of Atheism* (Grand Rapids: Baker, 2004).

# 3 | Does Morality Need God?

If God does not exist, then objective moral values—values that are valid and binding whether anybody believes in them or not—do not exist. Thus to say, for example, that the Holocaust was objectively wrong is to say that it was wrong even though the Nazis who carried it out thought that it was right and that it would still have been wrong even if the Nazis had won World War II and succeeded in exterminating or brainwashing everyone who disagreed with them. Now if God does not exist, then moral values are not objective in this way. Many theists and atheists alike concur on this point.

## ■ OPEN

Tell about a time you tried to convince someone that you hadn't done something wrong, even though you had.

Now, as an adult, do you think some actions are always wrong? Why or why not?

## ■ STUDY

Though recently somewhat politicized, the Ten Commandments have long been regarded as among the most significant moral codes ever penned. Yet this document is more than a list of do's and don'ts. After God revealed his name to Moses, he delivered

the people of Israel from the bondage of Egypt (the "Exodus")
and led toward the land he promised them. Much like the giving
of marriage vows, God then made a covenant with them—the
Ten Commandments—in the desert at Mount Sinai so that they
would remember him and his promises. **Read Exodus 20:1-17.**

*¹And God spoke all these words:*

*²"I am the LORD your God, who brought you out of Egypt, out of the*
*land of slavery.*

*³You shall have no other gods before me.*

*⁴You shall not make for yourself an idol in the form of anything in*
*heaven above or on the earth beneath or in the waters below. ⁵You*
*shall not bow down to them or worship them; for I, the LORD your*
*God, am a jealous God, punishing the children for the sin of the fa-*
*thers to the third and fourth generation of those who hate me, ⁶but*
*showing love to a thousand generations of those who love me and*
*keep my commandments.*

*⁷You shall not misuse the name of the LORD your God, for the LORD*
*will not hold anyone guiltless who misuses his name.*

*⁸Remember the Sabbath day by keeping it holy. ⁹Six days you shall la-*
*bor and do all your work, ¹⁰but the seventh day is a Sabbath to the*
*LORD your God. On it you shall not do any work, neither you, nor*
*your son or daughter, nor your manservant or maidservant, nor*
*your animals, nor the alien within your gates. ¹¹For in six days the*
*LORD made the heavens and the earth, the sea, and all that is in*
*them, but he rested on the seventh day. Therefore the LORD blessed*
*the Sabbath day and made it holy.*

*¹²Honor your father and your mother, so that you may live long in the*
*land the LORD your God is giving you.*

*¹³You shall not murder.*

*¹⁴You shall not commit adultery.*

*¹⁵You shall not steal.*

*¹⁶You shall not give false testimony against your neighbor.*

*¹⁷You shall not covet your neighbor's house. You shall not covet your neighbor's wife, or his manservant or maidservant, his ox or donkey, or anything that belongs to your neighbor."*

**1.** Notice what God says before he gives the people the Ten Commandments (verse 2). Why do you think he says this? What does it reveal about him?

**2.** How does God's covenant relationship with the Israelites (verse 2) inform the meaning of the first two commandments (verses 3-6)?

**3.** The fourth commandment says, "Remember the Sabbath day by keeping it holy" (verse 8). Where do you turn to remind yourself of your commitments?

**4.** What do you find most challenging in human relationships? How do the final three commandments (verses 15-17) sum up much of our daily interaction with neighbors and family?

I don't see any reason to think that in the absence of God, the herd morality evolved by Homo sapiens is objective. After all, if there is no God, then what's so special about human beings? They're just accidental by-products of nature which have evolved relatively recently on an infinitesimal speck of dust lost somewhere in a hostile and mindless universe and which are doomed to perish individually and collectively in a relatively short time. On the atheistic view, some action, say, rape, may not be socially advantageous, and so in the course of human development has become taboo; but that does absolutely nothing to prove that rape is really wrong. On the atheistic view, there's nothing really *wrong* with your raping someone.

(In fact, it is quite conceivable that rape could have evolved as an action advantageous for the survival of the species.) Thus, without God there is no absolute right and wrong which imposes itself on our conscience.

But the problem is that objective values do exist, and deep down we all know it. There's no more reason to deny the objective reality of moral values than the objective reality of the physical world.

**5.** Some atheists and skeptics argue that we do not need God to be good. How does the passage above respond?

**6.** Why does atheism fail to show that a heinous act such as rape or murder is absolutely wrong?

**7.** "Deep down we all know that objective moral values exist."
Would you agree? Why or why not?

Moral evil in the world does not disprove God's goodness; on
the contrary it actually *proves* it. For we may argue:

1. If God does not exist, objective moral values do not exist.
2. Evil exists.
3. Therefore, objective moral values exist (some things are
   truly evil).
4. Therefore, God exists.

Thus, evil paradoxically proves God's existence, since without God things would not be good or evil. Notice that this argument thus shows the compatibility of God and evil
without giving a clue as to *why* God permits evil. That is a
wholly separate question. But even in the absence of any answer to the why question, the present argument proves that
evil does not call into question, but actually requires, God's
existence.

**8.** The moral argument seems to be the most obvious argument
for the existence of God. Explain why God must exist if objective moral values exist.

**9.** Look again at question 2. If there is a God, what difference does it make that he reveals his moral law in the context of an intimate relationship like marriage?

Does this knowledge change your understanding of the Ten Commandments and/or of God?

**10.** What is one surprising thought that has come to you during this study?

# ■ GOING FURTHER

Give further thought to questions 2 and 3, and as you feel comfortable, consider talking to someone about your response.

### Additional Reading

For one of the best discussions on the question of objective moral values, see "Right and Wrong as a Clue to the Meaning in the Universe," the first section of C. S. Lewis's classic book *Mere Christianity.*

# 4 | Can Naturalism Make Sense of the Universe?

PSALM 104:1–18, 24–32

There is so much intelligibility and specified complexity in this world that it seems willful and prejudiced to try to explain it away with no intelligence behind it. Can morality, personality, and reality be reasonably explained without a personal, moral, first cause? How does one explain some of the features of a garden apart from there being a gardener? What kind of proof for a gardener will suffice anyway? What if the gardener did come and was seen and desires that our trust in his work not be dependent on only a direct sighting of him, because the essence of our relationship is not the constancy of sight and intervention, but the steadfastness of trust and sufficiency?"[1]

## ■ OPEN

Describe a beautiful garden you have seen. What elements make it beautiful? What tasks might, if left unattended, cause someone to wonder whether a gardener tended it?

---

[1]Ravi Zacharias, *Jesus Among Other Gods* (Nashville: Word Publishing, 2000), p. 167.

# ■ STUDY

Psalm 104 is a creation song. The psalmist ascribes the beauty, boundaries and provisions of the earth and its creatures to a loving and attentive Creator. The writer considers the days of creation in Genesis 1 and structures his verse similarly. **Read Psalm 104:1-18.**

[1]*Praise the LORD, O my soul.*

   *O LORD my God, you are very great;*

   *you are clothed with splendor and majesty.*

[2]*He wraps himself in light as with a garment;*

   *he stretches out the heavens like a tent*

[3]*and lays the beams of his upper chambers on their waters.*

   *He makes the clouds his chariot*

   *and rides on the wings of the wind.*

[4]*He makes winds his messengers,*

   *flames of fire his servants.*

[5]*He set the earth on its foundations;*

   *it can never be moved.*

[6]*You covered it with the deep as with a garment;*

   *the waters stood above the mountains.*

[7]*But at your rebuke the waters fled,*

   *at the sound of your thunder they took to flight;*

[8]*they flowed over the mountains,*

   *they went down into the valleys,*

   *to the place you assigned for them.*

[9]*You set a boundary they cannot cross;*

   *never again will they cover the earth.*

[10]*He makes springs pour water into the ravines;*

it flows between the mountains.
[11]They give water to all the beasts of the field;
    the wild donkeys quench their thirst.
[12]The birds of the air nest by the waters;
    they sing among the branches.
[13]He waters the mountains from his upper chambers;
    the earth is satisfied by the fruit of his work.
[14]He makes grass grow for the cattle,
    and plants for man to cultivate—
    bringing forth food from the earth:
[15]wine that gladdens the heart of man,
    oil to make his face shine,
    and bread that sustains his heart.
[16]The trees of the LORD are well watered,
    the cedars of Lebanon that he planted.
[17]There the birds make their nests;
    the stork has its home in the pine trees.
[18]The high mountains belong to the wild goats;
    the crags are a refuge for the coneys.

**1.** In verses 1 and 2, with what does the psalmist envision God as being clothed?

**2.** Verses 2-4 vividly personify God in a unique manner. Describe this scene.

**3.** How would you describe the tone of this psalm? Fearful? Joyful? Reverent?

**4.** Observe the relationship between God and the universe that we find in this passage, namely the action portrayed. Does this language match your understanding of God and our world? Why or why not?

**Consider the following parable from Antony Flew:**

Once upon a time two explorers came upon a clearing in the jungle. In the clearing were growing many flowers and many weeds. One explorer says, "Some gardener must tend this plot." The other disagrees, "There is no gardener." So they pitch their tents and set a watch. No gardener is ever seen. "But perhaps he is an invisible gardener." So they set up a barbed-wire fence. They electrify it. They patrol it with bloodhounds. (For they remember how H. G. Wells' *The Invisible Man* could be both smelt and touched though he could not be seen.) But no shrieks ever suggested that some intruder has received a shock. No movements of the wire ever betray an invisible climber. The bloodhounds never give cry. Yet still the Believer is not convinced. "But there is a gardener, invisible, intangible, insensible to electric shocks, a gardener who has no scent and makes no sound, a gardener who comes secretly to look after the garden which he loves." At last

> the Skeptic despairs, "But what remains of your original assertion? Just how does what you call an invisible, intangible, eternally elusive gardener differ from an imaginary gardener or even from no gardener at all?"[2]
>
> Flew is a naturalist. He holds that the concept of there being a supernatural being passes beyond the realm of where things make sense.

**5.** What do naturalists believe about the source of nature?

**6.** According to this parable, why does Antony Flew doubt God's existence?

### Read Psalm 104:24-32.

[24]*How many are your works, O LORD!*

*In wisdom you made them all;*

*the earth is full of your creatures.*

[25]*There is the sea, vast and spacious,*

*teeming with creatures beyond number—*

*living things both large and small.*

[26]*There the ships go to and fro,*

*and the leviathan, which you formed to frolic there.*

[27]*These all look to you*

*to give them their food at the proper time.*

---

[2]Antony Flew in *New Essays in Philosophical Theology,* ed. Antony Flew and Alasdair MacIntyre (London: SCM Press, 1955), p. 96.

$^{28}$When you give it to them,
> they gather it up;
> when you open your hand,
> they are satisfied with good things.

$^{29}$When you hide your face,
> they are terrified;
> when you take away their breath,
> they die and return to the dust.

$^{30}$When you send your Spirit,
> they are created,
> and you renew the face of the earth.

$^{31}$May the glory of the LORD endure forever;
> may the LORD rejoice in his works—

$^{32}$he who looks at the earth, and it trembles,
> who touches the mountains, and they smoke.

**7.** Notice the words the psalmist associates with God's works in verses 24 and 31. What do these words tell us about God and about his creation?

**8.** Typical of poetry, this psalm personifies the world as having an intimate and responsive relationship with God. Describe the aspects of this relationship depicted in verses 27-30 and verse 32.

Is *every* aspect of a human gardener observable? Sure, one sees Pat Doe, the visible gardener, going about her work, but what of Pat's intentions, desires, sensations and thoughts? These may be *inferred* or *embodied* in the sense that Pat expresses her intent to plant tomatoes, that she acts on this intention and so on. But are her thoughts—her *consciousness*—visible or observable?

Materialists face a problem in explaining the emergence of consciousness. As one naturalist writes:

> Consider the universe before conscious beings came along: the odds did not look good that such beings could come to exist. We have a good idea how the Big Bang led to the creation of stars and galaxies, principally by force of gravity. But we know of no comparable force that might explain how ever-expanding lumps of matter might have developed an inner conscious life.[3]

Theism does not see consciousness as an anomaly but as something that is at the very heart of reality. The existence of consciousness remains a thorn in the side of naturalism, and a clue to a comprehensive theism.

9. The existence of consciousness remains a thorn in the side of naturalism because naturalism has no plausible explanation for how consciousness could come into being without an intelligent designer. How does this insight point to a personal God and Creator?

---

[3]Colin McGinn, *The Mysterious Flame: Conscious Minds in a Material World* (New York: Basic Books, 2000), pp. 14-15.

**10.** Antony Flew recently announced that he now believes that God *must* exist. Given our study thus far, how does this knowledge surprise you? encourage you?

■ **GOING FURTHER**

Take time to journal about Flew's parable above and reply to it. Or, if you have read C. S. Lewis, consider how he might have responded to the parable.

**Additional Reading**

Read or revisit C. S. Lewis's *The Lion, the Witch and the Wardrobe* and observe each of the children's different responses to the idea of a country beyond the wardrobe. Note how Peter's and Susan's initial arguments resemble Antony Flew's. Consider why Edmund's resistance remains long after he encounters this country while others are immediately changed by their encounters.

## 5 | Is God Knowable?

PSALM 34:4-10
HEBREWS 11:1-3, 6

We can know that God exists wholly apart from arguments simply by immediately experiencing him. This was the way people described in the Bible knew God. For these people God was not inferred to be the best explanation of their religious experience and so they believed in him; rather, in their religious experience they came to know God *directly.*

### ■ OPEN

Talk about a relationship that moved from casual to personal— the first time, for example, you really took notice of your spouse-to-be or a dear friend. How did your feelings toward the person change? What prompted the change?

### ■ STUDY

The Scriptures contend that the one who seeks God earnestly will find him. The following selections from Psalm 34 and Hebrews 11 describe a God who not only is knowable but *desires* to be known. The psalm is written by David, who thanks God for responding to his prayers by providing him deliverance and wisdom. David depicts this wisdom as relational: It is an intimate knowledge, a reverence ("fear") and love of God. The writer of Hebrews offers a similar perspective of the one seeking God, and here, faith is characterized as relational. **Read Psalm 34:4-10.**

*⁴I sought the LORD, and he answered me;*
   *he delivered me from all my fears.*
*⁵Those who look to him are radiant;*
   *their faces are never covered with shame.*
*⁶This poor man called, and the LORD heard him;*
   *he saved him out of all his troubles.*
*⁷The angel of the LORD encamps around those who fear him,*
   *and he delivers them.*
*⁸Taste and see that the LORD is good;*
   *blessed is the man who takes refuge in him.*
*⁹Fear the LORD, you his saints,*
   *for those who fear him lack nothing.*
*¹⁰The lions may grow weak and hungry,*
   *but those who seek the LORD lack no good thing.*

**1.** What actions are mentioned in each of the first stanzas of verses 4-6?

What is God's response to them?

**2.** David links fearing God with seeking him and finding refuge in him. What do you think it means to fear God?

**3.** Do you sometimes struggle with the idea of God being good? When?

How might you "taste and see that the LORD is good" (verse 8)?

> Regarding the way people described in the Bible knew God, Professor John Hick explains,
>
> > God was known to them as a dynamic will interacting with their own wills, a sheer given reality, as inescapably to be reckoned with as destructive storm and life-giving sunshine. . . . They did not think of God as an inferred entity but as an experienced reality. . . . To them God was not a proposition completing a syllogism, or an idea adopted by the mind, but the experiential reality which gave significance to their lives.[4]
>
> Philosophers call beliefs like this "properly basic beliefs." They aren't based on some other beliefs; rather they are part of the foundation of a person's system of beliefs. Other properly basic beliefs would be the belief in the reality of the past, the existence of the external world and the presence of other

---

[4]John Hick, ed., *The Existence of God*, Problems of Philosophy Series (New York: Macmillan, 1964), pp. 13-14.

minds like your own. When you think about it, none of these beliefs can be proved. How could you prove that the world was not created five minutes ago with built-in appearances of age like food in our stomachs from the breakfasts we never really ate and memory traces in our brains of events we never really experienced? How could you prove that you are not a brain in a vat of chemicals being stimulated with electrodes by some mad scientist?

Although these sorts of beliefs are basic for us, that doesn't mean that they're arbitrary. Rather they are grounded in the sense that they're formed in the context of certain experiences. In the experiential context of seeing and feeling and hearing things, I naturally form the belief that there are certain physical objects which I am sensing. Thus, my basic beliefs are not arbitrary, but appropriately grounded in experience. There may be no way to prove such beliefs, and yet it is perfectly rational to hold them. You would have to be crazy to think that the world was created five minutes ago or to believe that you are a brain in a vat! Such beliefs are thus not merely basic, but *properly* basic.

In the same way, belief in God is for those who seek him a properly basic belief grounded in our experience of God, as we discern him in nature, conscience and other means.

**4.** In what way did people in the Bible know God?

How does their knowledge differ from a casual observer's or, for example, from someone studying the solar system?

**5.** According to the passage above, why is belief in God "properly basic"?

Why are such beliefs not able to be proved?

> Now if, through experiencing God, we can know in a properly basic way that God exists, then there's a real danger that proofs for God could actually distract one's attention from God himself. If you're sincerely seeking God, God will make his existence evident to you. The Bible promises, "Draw near to God and he will draw near to you" (James 4:8). We mustn't so concentrate on the proofs for God that we fail to hear the inner voice of God to our own heart. For those who listen, God becomes an immediate reality in their lives.

**6.** How might the focus on proofs for God's existence actually distract you from the knowledge of God?

**7.** The Scriptures affirm that God will draw near to those who draw near to him. How may you begin (or continue) to do this today or this week?

**Read Hebrews 11:1-3, 6.**

¹*Now faith is being sure of what we hope for and certain of what we do not see.* ²*This is what the ancients were commended for.* ³*By faith we understand that the universe was formed at God's command, so that what is seen was not made out of what was visible.* . . . ⁶*And without faith it is impossible to please God, because anyone who comes to him must believe that he exists and that he rewards those who earnestly seek him.*

**8.** What is the definition of faith given here? Is it tenuous or certain?

**9.** Consider the relationship between faith and knowing God. In what ways do relationships require faith or a committed trust in another?

**10.** Why do you think believing that God "rewards those who earnestly seek him" is necessary to knowing him?

What does this belief tell us about his character (indifferent, generous, begrudging)?

**11.** Do you have a sense that you really know God? How might you get to know him in a more intimate way?

## ■ GOING FURTHER

Write out your thoughts about the idea that God is knowable and rewards those who earnestly seek after him. You might want to spend some time reading through Psalm 34 and even praying that God would reveal himself in a more intimate way.

### Additional Reading

For a classic book on this topic, see J. I. Packer's *Knowing God* (Downers Grove, Ill.: InterVarsity Press, 1993).

## 6 | What Difference Does God Make?

JOHN 1:1-18

We need to take seriously the ways in which God may be so much greater than what our language, pictures and metaphors can point to. This is fundamental to appreciate, lest we become more interested in our idea of God than in the reality of God itself—a mistake that would be as ill-suited as a lover being more enamored by the *idea* of the beloved rather than the *beloved*. The lover needs some idea of the beloved in order for there to be any specific shape to his or her love, but the whole point of having such an idea is for there to be a loving exchange. Philosophical reflection on the idea of God, like philosophical reflection on the idea of love, can set the stage for, but not replace, an exchange on another, deeper level.

### ■ OPEN

Tell about a book (fiction or non-fiction) that was life-transforming for you. What ideas or characters did you encounter? Why did they make such an impact on you?

### ■ STUDY

The apostle John, an intimate friend and disciple of Jesus, is the author of the Gospel that bears his name. At the close of his Gos-

pel, he tells his readers why he wrote it: "Jesus did many other
miraculous signs in the presence of his disciples, which are not
recorded in this book. But these are written that you may believe
that Jesus is the Christ, the Son of God, and that by believing you
may have life in his name" (John 20:30-31). The disciple's opening words speak of the One who came to give us such knowledge
of God, or as he puts it, "life in his name." **Read John 1:1-18.**

*¹In the beginning was the Word, and the Word was with God, and the
Word was God. ²He was with God in the beginning.*

*³Through him all things were made; without him nothing was made
that has been made. ⁴In him was life, and that life was the light of
men. ⁵The light shines in the darkness, but the darkness has not understood it.*

*⁶There came a man who was sent from God; his name was John.
⁷He came as a witness to testify concerning that light, so that through
him all men might believe. ⁸He himself was not the light; he came only
as a witness to the light. ⁹The true light that gives light to every man
was coming into the world.*

*¹⁰He was in the world, and though the world was made through
him, the world did not recognize him. ¹¹He came to that which was his
own, but his own did not receive him. ¹²Yet to all who received him, to
those who believed in his name, he gave the right to become children
of God—¹³children born not of natural descent, nor of human deci-
sion or a husband's will, but born of God.*

*¹⁴The Word became flesh and made his dwelling among us. We
have seen his glory, the glory of the One and Only, who came from the
Father, full of grace and truth.*

*¹⁵John testifies concerning him. He cries out, saying, "This was he
of whom I said, 'He who comes after me has surpassed me because he*

*was before me.'"* ¹⁶*From the fullness of his grace we have all received one blessing after another.* ¹⁷*For the law was given through Moses; grace and truth came through Jesus Christ.* ¹⁸*No one has ever seen God, but God the One and Only, who is at the Father's side, has made him known.*

**1.** Think back to Genesis 1 in the first session. What echoes from that passage of Scripture do you hear in verses 1 and 2?

**2.** What further insight does John give into the creation story in verses 3 and 10?

**3.** John uses one word seven times in verses 4-9. What emotions or thoughts do you associate with the repetition of this word? Why?

**4.** Verses 14 and 15 describe a unique event called the *incarnation*. What does John tell us about this event?

The key to the paradox or mystery of the incarnation (and I agree that there will always remain mystery) is in recognizing that while Christianity holds that Jesus Christ is both human and divine, Christ is not the entirety of the divine. Christ is traditionally described as *totus deus* (wholly God), not *totum dei* (the whole of God). Because of the vastness or infinity of God, God can be all-knowing as the unincarnate, overarching divine Creator and be finite and not all-knowing as a human being. By tradition, the incarnation does not involve an infinite, all knowing, all powerful God ceasing to be God. Rather, it involves God including, enveloping or becoming incarnate ("enfleshed") finite, human life.

The coherence of the incarnation may be more richly appreciated when one takes into account the overall Christian conception of the cosmos. According to Christianity, human beings are made in the image of God. Because of this, humans are believed to resemble God in certain limited ways. Thus, while the incarnation involves God taking on a nature that is *distinct* from God, it involves God taking on a nature which *stems* from God's nature.

An additional point needs to be made. Sometimes the resistance to the incarnation stems from an exceedingly low view of the value of human beings. Humanity may well appear to be hopelessly wicked and flawed at almost every level. Against this, a central Christian conviction is that wickedness is an injury to our nature; evil is dysfunctional. This dysfunction may be normal, habitual and routine. In fact, most Christians believe we all have some share in this dysfunction or, to use religious language, sin. In the incarnation Christians believe that our humanity is shown to be fulfilled in Christ's wisdom, love and sacrificial action in finite, concrete ways. Our broken humanity is to be healed, renewed and ultimately resurrected with Christ.

**5.** How does our identity as human beings help us to further understand the incarnation?

**6.** Jesus' incarnation addresses the problem of evil as no other worldview does or can. Explain.

**7.** Look back at the passage from John's Gospel. What does the writer mean by the words "received" and "believed"? Restate his thought in these verses.

**8.** What do verses 16 and 17 tell us about Jesus and his ministry?

**9.** John employs a descriptive phrase in verses 14 and 18 (found also in John 3:16). What does this phrase communicate about Jesus? Does this description intrigue, confuse or perhaps unsettle you? Explain.

**10.** What is the point of reflecting on the idea of God? What purpose does it serve?

**11.** Based on the assertions of this study, what does it mean to *know* God?

Today, how might you begin or continue to know God on a deeper level?

## ■ GOING FURTHER

Take time to read through the entire Gospel of John, ideally in one sitting. Underline or note the way Jesus speaks of his relationship with God and his mission.

### Additional Reading

Ravi Zacharias examines the Gospel of John in his compelling study of Jesus, *Jesus Among Other Gods* (Nashville: Word, 2000).

# Leader's Notes

Leading a small group discussion can be an enjoyable and rewarding experience. But it can also be *scary*—especially if you've never done it before. If this is your feeling, you're in good company. When God asked Moses to lead the Israelites out of Egypt, he replied, "O LORD, please send someone else to do it" (Ex 4:13). It was the same with Solomon, Jeremiah and Timothy, but God helped these people in spite of their weaknesses, and he will help you as well.

You don't need to be an expert on the Bible or a trained teacher to lead a group discussion. The idea behind these studies is that the leader guides group members in their exploration of critical questions in the life of faith. This method of learning will allow group members to remember much more of what is said than a lecture would.

These studies are designed to be led easily. As a matter of fact, the flow of questions is so natural that you may feel that the studies lead themselves. This study guide is also flexible. You can use it with a variety of groups—student, professional, neighborhood or church groups. Each study takes around sixty minutes in a group setting.

There are some important facts to know about group dynamics and encouraging discussion. The suggestions listed below should enable you to effectively and enjoyably fulfill your role as leader.

## ■ PREPARING FOR THE STUDY

1. Ask God to help you understand and apply the material in each session for your own life. Unless this happens, you will not be prepared to lead others. Pray too for the various members of the group. Ask God to open your hearts to the message of his Word and motivate you to action.

2. Read the introduction to the entire guide to get an overview of the entire book and the issues which will be explored.

3. As you begin each study, read and reread the assigned material to familiarize yourself with it.

4. Carefully work through each question in the study. Spend time in meditation and reflection as you consider how to respond.

5. Write your thoughts and responses in the space provided in the study guide. This will help you to express your understanding of the material clearly.

6. It might help to have a Bible dictionary handy. Use it to look up any unfamiliar words, names or places. (For additional help on how to study a passage, see chapter five of *How to Lead a LifeGuide Bible Study*, InterVarsity Press.)

7. Consider how the Scripture applies to your life. Remember that the group will follow your lead in responding to the studies. They will not go any deeper than you do.

8. Once you have finished your own study of the passage, familiarize yourself with the leader's notes for the study you are leading. These are designed to help you in several ways. First, they tell you the purpose the study guide author had in mind when writing the study. Take time to think through how the study questions work together to accomplish that purpose. Second, the notes provide you with additional background information for various questions. This infor-

mation can be useful when people have difficulty understanding or answering a question. Third, the leader's notes can alert you to potential problems you may encounter during the study.

**9.** If you wish to remind yourself of anything mentioned in the leader's notes, make a note to yourself below that question in the study.

## ■ LEADING THE STUDY

**1.** Begin the study on time. Open with prayer, asking God to help the group to understand and apply the material being discussed.

**2.** Be sure that everyone in your group has a study guide. Encourage the group to prepare beforehand for each discussion by reading the introduction to the guide and by working through the questions in that week's session.

**3.** At the beginning of your first time together, explain that these studies are meant to be discussions, not lectures. Encourage the members of the group to participate. However, do not put pressure on those who may be hesitant to speak during the first few sessions. You may want to suggest the following guidelines to your group.

• Stick to the topic being discussed.

• Your responses should be based on the material provided and not on outside authorities such as commentaries or speakers.

• Only rarely should you refer to other portions of the Bible. This allows for everyone to participate in in-depth study on equal ground.

• Anything said in the group is considered confidential and will not be discussed outside the group unless specific permission is given to do so.

• We will listen attentively to each other and provide time for each person present to talk.

• We will pray for each other.

4. Have a group member read the introduction at the beginning of the discussion.

5. Every session begins with a group discussion question. The question or activity is meant to be used before the passage is read. The question introduces the theme of the study and encourages group members to begin to open up. Encourage as many members as possible to participate, and be ready to get the discussion going with your own response.

   This section is designed to reveal where our thoughts or feelings need to be transformed by the renewing of our minds. That is why it is especially important not to read the passage to the group members before the discussion question is asked. The passage will tend to color the honest reactions people would otherwise give because they are, of course, supposed to think the way the Bible does.

   You may want to supplement the group discussion question with an icebreaker to help people to get comfortable. See the community section of *Small Group Idea Book* for more ideas.

6. Have a group member (or members if the passage is long) read aloud the textual material as it occurs in the session. Then give people several minutes to read the passage again silently so that they can take it all in.

7. As you ask the questions, keep in mind that they are designed to be used just as they are written. You may simply read them aloud. Or you may prefer to express them in your own words. There may be times when it is appropriate to deviate from the study guide. For example, a question may have already been answered. If so, move on to the next question. Or someone may raise an important question not covered in the guide. Take time to discuss it, but try to keep the group from going off on tangents.

8. Avoid answering your own questions. If necessary, repeat or rephrase them until they are clearly understood. Or point out something you read in the leader's notes to clarify the context or meaning. An eager group quickly becomes passive and silent if they think the leader will do most of the talking.

9. Don't be afraid of silence. People may need time to think about the question before formulating their answers.

10. Don't be content with just one answer. Ask, "What do the rest of you think?" or "Anything else?" until several people have given answers to the question.

11. Acknowledge all contributions. Try to be affirming whenever possible. Never reject an answer. If it is clearly off-base, ask, "Which verse led you to that conclusion?" or again, "What do the rest of you think?"

12. Don't expect every answer to be addressed to you, even though this will probably happen at first. As group members become more at ease, they will begin to truly interact with each other. This is one sign of healthy discussion.

13. Don't be afraid of controversy. It can be very stimulating. If you don't resolve an issue completely, don't be frustrated. Move on and keep it in mind for later. A subsequent study may solve the problem.

14. Periodically summarize what the group has said to that point. This helps to draw together the various ideas mentioned and gives continuity to the discussion. But don't preach.

15. Give an opportunity during the session for people to talk about what they are learning.

16. Conclude your time together with conversational prayer. Ask for

God's help in working through the implications of the discussion.

**17.** End on time.

## ■ COMPONENTS OF SMALL GROUPS

A healthy small group should do more than study the Bible. There are four components to consider as you structure your time together.

- *Nurture.* Small groups help us to grow in our knowledge and love of God. Bible study is the key to making this happen and is the foundation of your small group.

- *Community.* Small groups are a great place to develop deep friendships with other Christians. Allow time for informal interaction before and after each discussion. Plan activities and games that will help you get to know each other. Spend time having fun together—going on a picnic or cooking dinner together.

- *Worship and prayer.* Your study will be enhanced by spending time praising God together in prayer or song. Pray for each other's needs— and keep track of how God is answering prayer in your group. Ask God to help you to apply what you are learning in your study.

- *Outreach.* Reaching out to others can be a practical way of applying what you are learning, and it will keep your group from becoming self-focused. Host a series of evangelistic discussions for your friends or neighbors. Clean up the yard of an elderly friend. Serve at a soup kitchen together, or spend a day working on a Habitat house.

Many more suggestions and helps in each of these areas are found in *Small Group Idea Book.* Information on building a small group can be found in *Small Group Leaders' Handbook* and *The Big Book on Small Groups* (both from InterVarsity Press). Reading through one of these books would be worth your time.

## STUDY 1

# Who or What Made God?

ISAIAH 40:12-14, 18-28

*Purpose:* **To show the idea of an eternal, self-existent God is reasonable and best explains our understanding of the world.**

**QUESTIONS 1-3.** Five times in this passage Isaiah asks a rhetorical question to cause us to pause and consider what we mean when we speak of "God." The answer: He is the all-powerful creator who knows the precise measurement and weight of the waters and the mountains. He is all-wise and no one is able to offer him knowledge or understanding of which he is not aware. These questions echo the very questions God asks Job (see Job 38—41) when he is overwhelmed by grief and stunned by God's seeming silence. On the surface these questions may seem harsh to those in enslavement (Isaiah's audience) or reeling from devastating loss (Job). However, both texts underscore that God is not only the sovereign, majestic One to whom none can compare but that He is compassionate and attentive: He hears and responds to the cries of his people. Indeed, Job and the Israelites plea for an audience with God and God *shows up*, proclaiming "Comfort, comfort my people... Speak tenderly to Jerusalem" (Is 40:1). The writer of Job puts it more starkly, "Then the Lord answered Job out of the storm" (Job 38:1).

**QUESTIONS 4-5.** Many who doubt or do not believe in God's existence think that science has essentially disproved his reality. Since God cannot be examined in a laboratory, he must be only imaginary. Ravi Zacharias comments on this erroneous conclusion: "A neurophysiologist studies the brain (just one intricate strand of study), with its billion long nerve cells, each of which, on the average, makes contact with 10,000 other cells under the control of chemical messengers. Even the brain of an octopus far exceeds in complexity any human artifact, and the human brain is immensely more complex. . . .

"This is the magnitude of information from just one physical organ, thus hardly a pursuit for a hobbyist at play. When one adds the other dimensions of a human being's intricate nature, the task is no longer manageable by the physical scientist alone. Humans also function as social and aesthetic beings. Our unique linguistic capacities, our moral struggles, our religious bent, our yearning for love, and our search for personhood only add to the endeavor at hand. This complexity necessitates that scientific theorizing recognize its own limitations, or the conclusions will be severely warped" (Ravi Zacharias, *The Real Face of Atheism* [Grand Rapids: Baker, 2004], pp. 39-40).

**QUESTION 6.** Once again Isaiah examines God's identity and significance with a question of comparison: "To whom, then, will you compare God?" (vv. 18 and 25). The prophet reminds his audience that the God of Israel stands in stark contrast to the gods of Babylon and other nations. "In the ancient world the gods were viewed as having human weaknesses and often were inattentive or simply unaware of events that were taking place. One result of this was the pantheon of gods were constantly outwitting and tricking each other. . . . The gods were not indefatigable. They were in constant need of food, drink, and shelter. In fact, humans were created to do the hard labor the gods preferred not to do" (John H. Walton, Victor H. Matthews and Mark W. Chavalas, *The IVP Bible Background Commentary: Old Testament* [Downers Grove, Ill.: InterVarsity Press, 2000], p. 627).

**QUESTION 7.** Unlike creation and all other reality, God is self-existent and was not created. Norman Geisler comments, "Traditionally, most atheists who deny the existence of God believe that the universe was not made; it was just 'there' forever. They appeal to the first law of thermodynamics for support: 'Energy can neither be created nor destroyed,' they insist. Several things must be observed in response.

"First, this way of stating the first law is not scientific; rather, it is a philosophical assertion. Science is based on observation, and there is no observational evidence that can support the dogmatic 'can' and 'cannot' in this statement. It should read, '[As far as we have observed,] the amount of actual energy in the universe remains constant.' That is, no one has observed any actual new energy either coming into existence or going out of existence. Once the first law is understood properly, it says nothing about the universe being eternal or having no beginning. As far as the first law is concerned, energy may or may not have been created. It simply asserts that if energy was created, then as far as we can tell, the actual amount of energy that was created has remained constant since then.

"Further, let us suppose for the sake of argument that energy—the whole universe of energy we call the cosmos—was not created, as many atheists have traditionally believed. If this is so, then it is meaningless to ask who made the universe. If energy is eternal and uncreated, then of course no one created it. It has always existed. However, if it is meaningless to ask, 'Who made the universe?' since it has always existed, then it is equally meaningless to ask, 'Who made God?' since he has always existed.

"If the universe is not eternal, it needs a cause. On the other hand, if it has no beginning, it does not need a cause of its beginning. Likewise, if a God exists who has no beginning, it is absurd to ask 'Who made God?' It is a category mistake to ask, 'Who made the Unmade?' or 'Who created the Uncreated?' One may as well ask, 'Where is the bachelor's wife?' " (Norman Geisler, "Who Made God?" in *Who Made God? And Answers to Over 100 Tough Questions of Faith,* ed. Ravi Zacharias and Norman Geisler [Grand Rapids: Zondervan, 2003], pp. 23-24).

**QUESTION 9.** This question will be examined further in the next section, but consider William Lane Craig's observation (also quoted in the next study): "During the last thirty years or so, scientists have discovered that the existence of intelligent life like ours depends upon a complex and delicate balance of initial conditions given in the Big Bang itself. Scientists once believed that whatever the initial conditions of the universe, eventually intelligent life might evolve. But we now know that our existence is balanced on a knife's edge. It seems vastly more probable that a life-*prohibiting* universe rather than a life-*permitting* universe like ours should exist. The existence of intelligent life depends upon a conspiracy of initial conditions which must be fine-tuned to a degree that is literally incomprehensible and incalculable. For example, Stephen Hawking has estimated that if the rate of the universe's expansion one second after the Big Bang had been smaller by even one part in a hundred thousand million million, the universe would have re-collapsed into a hot fireball."

## STUDY 2

# Does God Make Sense of the Universe?

GENESIS 1

*Purpose:* **To suggest that the origin and complexity of the universe can only be explained by a God who created it.**

**QUESTION 1.** As many scholars have noted, the phrase "formless and empty" is the opposite of "heavens and the earth" in verse 1. "The earth is a dark abyss, inhospitable to life," writes Bruce K. Waltke in *Genesis: A Commentary* ([Grand Rapids: Zondervan, 2001], p. 60). In contrast to this emptiness we are introduced to the Spirit of God "hovering over the waters," as God the Father calls light and the rest of creation into being.

**QUESTION 2.** In his classic work *I Believe in the Holy Spirit,* Oxford scholar and RZIM associate Michael Green writes, "The word used for the Spirit of God in both Hebrew and Greek is highly significant. *Ruach* in Hebrew and *Pneuma* in Greek have the three main meanings of 'wind', 'breath' and 'spirit'. The Spirit of God is his life-giving breath without which man remains spiritually inert. It is his mysterious wind, which man cannot get under his tidy control: as Nicodemus was reminded by

Jesus, 'The wind (*pneuma*) blows where it will, and you will hear its sound but you do not know where it comes from or where it is going. So it is with every one who is born of the Spirit (*pneuma*)' (John 3:8). As well as being mysterious the wind is powerful: it was by a mighty wind that God assuaged the waters of the Flood (Genesis 8:1), and by a wind that he caused the waters to recede before Israel at the Exodus (Exodus 14:21). Those twin notions of power and mystery mark much of the teaching of Old and New Testaments alike when they treat of [Sic.] the Spirit of God" (*I Believe in the Holy Spirit,* rev. ed. [Grand Rapids: Eerdmans, 2004], p. 20).

**QUESTIONS 4-5.** Norman Geisler writes in *Who Made God?* "The famous agnostic Bertrand Russell presented this . . . dilemma: Either the world had a beginning, or it did not. If it did not, then it does not need a cause (God). If it did, we can ask, 'Who caused God?' But if God has a cause, he is not God. In either case, we do not arrive at a first uncaused cause (God).

"The answer to this tough question is that it, too, asks a meaningless question: Who made God? To put it another way, it wrongly assumes that *'everything* must have a cause' when what is claimed is that *'everything that had a beginning* had a cause.' This is quite a different matter. Of course, everything that had a beginning had a beginner. Nothing cannot make something" ("Who Made God?" pp. 24-25).

Similarly, the first premise does not state, "Whatever *exists* has a cause," but rather "Whatever *begins to exist* has a cause." The difference is important. The insight which lies at the root of premise (1) is that being cannot come from non-being, that something cannot come from nothing. God, since he never began to exist, would not require a cause, for he never came into being. Nor is this special pleading for God, since this is exactly what the atheist has always claimed about the universe: that it is eternal and uncaused. The problem is that the atheist's claim is now rendered untenable in light of the beginning of the universe.

**QUESTION 5.** For example, the cause of water's freezing is the temperature's being below 0° Centigrade. If the temperature were below 0° from eternity past, then any water that was around would be frozen from eternity. It would be impossible for the water to begin to freeze just a finite time ago. So if the cause is timelessly present, then the effect should be timelessly present as well. The only way for the cause to be timeless and the effect to begin in time is for the cause to be a personal agent who freely chooses to create an effect in time without any prior determining conditions. For example, a man sitting from eternity could freely will to stand up. Thus, we are brought, not merely to a transcendent cause of the universe, but to its personal creator.

**QUESTION 6.** "When God created people, he put them in charge of all of his creation. He endowed them with his own image. In the ancient world an image was believed to carry the essence of that which it represented. . . . In similar ways the governing work of God was seen to be accomplished by people. But that is not all there is to the image of God. Genesis 5:1-3 likens the image of God in Adam to the image of Adam in Seth. This goes beyond the comment about plants and animals reproducing after their own kind, though certainly children share physical characteristics and basic nature (genetically) with their parents. . . . The image provides the capacity not only to serve in the place of God (his representative containing his essence) but also to be and act like him. The tools he provided so that we may accomplish that task include conscience, self-awareness and spiritual discernment" (Walton, Matthews and Chavalas, *IVP Bible Background Commentary: Old Testament*, p. 29).

**QUESTION 7.** The writer uses "God" and "image" twice in this short poem, and "created" three times, emphasizing the significant event that takes place. The second stanza restates the first stanza, and the third stanza elaborates on being created in God's image: our male and female-ness reflect a personal, relational God.

Ravi Zacharias adds, "The principal thrust in the opening pages of Genesis is that God is the Creator and that He is both personal and eternal—He is a living, communicating God. The second is that the world did not come by accident but was designed with humanity in mind—man is an intelligent, spiritual being. The third thrust is that life could not be lived out alone but through companionship—man is a relational, dependent being. The fourth aspect is that man was fashioned as a moral entity with the privilege of self-determination—man is an accountable, rational being.

"Three significant relationships entail: that of man toward God—the sanctity of worship; that of man toward his spouse and fellow human beings—the sanctity of relationship; and that of man toward the created order—the sanctity of stewardship. Upon and from the first flow the other two" (Ravi Zacharias, *Jesus Among Other Gods* [Nashville: Word, 2000], p. 171).

**QUESTIONS 9-11.** It's important to understand that it's not just the probability that's at stake here. Any sequence of letters hammered out by a chimpanzee seated at a typewriter is equally improbable; but if we find a beautiful sonnet has been typed, then we know that this is not the result of blind chance, since it conforms to the independently given pattern of grammatical English sentences. In the same way, physics and biology tell us independently of any knowledge of the early conditions of the universe what the physical conditions requisite for life are. We then discover how incredibly improbable such conditions are. It is this combination of a specified pattern plus improbability that serves to render the chance hypothesis implausible.

With this in mind, we can immediately see the fallacy of those who say that the existence of any universe is equally improbable and therefore there is nothing here to be explained. It is not the improbability of some universe or others existing that concerns us; rather it is the specified probability of a life-permitting universe's existing that is at issue. Thus, the proper analogy to the fine-tuning of the universe is not, as defenders of the chance hypothesis often suppose, a lottery in which any individual's winning is fantastically and equally improbable but which some individual has to win. Rather the analogy is a lottery in which a single white ball is mixed into a billion billion billion black balls, and you are asked to reach in and pull out a ball. Any ball you pick will be equally improbable; nevertheless, it is overwhelmingly more probable that, whichever ball you pick, it will be black rather than white. Similarly, the existence of any particular universe is equally improbable; but it is incomprehensibly more probable that whichever universe exists, it will be life-prohibiting rather than life-permitting. It is the enormous, specified improbability of the fine-tuning that presents the hurdle for the chance hypothesis.

## STUDY 3
# Does Morality Need God?
EXODUS 20:1-23

*Purpose:* **To show that because objective moral values exist, God must also exist.**

**QUESTION 1.** Before God unveils his moral law, he announces who he is and what he has done for the people of Israel. "I am the LORD *your* God" (emphasis added), the One who has delivered his people from slavery in Egypt. This introduction is typical of other ancient covenants, in which the sovereign (the king) identifies himself and reiterates his record of provision for his people. Most significantly, the commands that follow are predicated upon the faithfulness of the king; the people entrust themselves to him in allegiance and obedience. Yet unlike other ancient sovereigns (Pharaoh, Nebuchadnezzar), the Lord God is faithful and worthy of trust and obedience.

**QUESTION 2.** A covenant is a binding promise between two parties, and implicit in such a bond—as in marriage—is a vow to exclusive love and faithfulness. Like one's marriage vows, God's covenant is more than a contract written on stone years ago. Rather, Scripture characterizes it as a life-sustaining promise and blessing of a relationship with the author himself, our Creator and Redeemer. When the Israelites suffered in Egypt, Exodus 2:24 says, "God heard their groaning and he remembered his covenant with Abraham, with Isaac and with Jacob." Just as he identifies himself as his people's Deliverer before he gives them the Ten Commandments, so he announces to Moses in Exodus 3:15-17, "Say to the Israelites, 'The LORD, the God of your fathers—the God of Abraham, the God of Isaac and the God of Jacob—has sent me to you.' This is my name forever, the name by which I am to be remembered from generation to generation. . . . I have watched over you and have seen what has been done to you in Egypt. And I have promised to bring you up out of your misery in Egypt."

We see first in these passages that God intimately associates his name with his people (the patriarchs) revealing that his covenant is a promise of enduring relationship. Second, his people—and thus, we ourselves—are exhorted to remember God. And third, we are assured that God will not overlook his people; he remembers his covenant and blesses those who hope in him.

**QUESTION 5.** Regarding the sense of meaninglessness that Nietzsche envisioned upon his "death of God" pronouncement, Ravi Zacharias writes, "In a sense, Nietzsche was the first western philosopher to face up fully to man's loss of faith in religion. He put down in black and white what many around him felt to be true, but were unwilling to acknowledge as the logical end of their belief. In pronouncing the death of God,

Nietzsche not only stepped right into the eye of the storm, he went further, and admitted that the storm clouds were even more devastating and violent than any of God's undertakers had imagined. The paralyzing darkness that fell was not so much an exterior phenomenon crowding inward, but rather, an inner blinding that spread outward. It was not just that the philosopher's sling had put out the lights; it was that the disorientation of the mind itself would not know whither to turn for light, and the result was terrifying. . . .

"The philosopher G. K. Chesterton said that to believe in the nonexistence of God would be analogous to waking up some morning, looking in the mirror, and seeing nothing. With no reflection, no perception, no idea whatsoever of the self, there would be nothing to conform to, and nothing to modify. Thus, the Socratic maxim, 'Know yourself,' would be rendered impossible" (Ravi Zacharias, *The Real Face of Atheism* [Grand Rapids: Baker, 2004], pp. 27-31).

**QUESTION 6.** Some atheist philosophers, unwilling to bite the bullet and affirm that acts like rape or torturing a child are morally neutral actions, have tried to affirm objective moral values in the absence of God. This "atheistic moral realism" affirms that moral values and duties do exist in reality and are not dependent upon evolution or human opinion, but atheistic moral realists insist that they are not grounded in God. Indeed, moral values have no further foundation. They just exist.

What does it mean to say, for example, that the moral value *justice* just exists? I don't know what this means. I understand what it is for a person to be just; but I draw a complete blank when it is said that, in the absence of any persons, *Justice* itself exists. Moral values seem to exist as properties of persons, not as abstractions—or at any rate, I don't know what it is for a moral value to exist as an abstraction.

Suppose that values like mercy, justice, love, forbearance and the like just exist. How does that result in any moral obligations for me? Why would I have a moral duty, say, to be merciful? Who or what lays such an obligation on me? As the ethicist Richard Taylor points out, "A duty is something that is owed. . . . But something can be owed only to some person or persons. There can be no such thing as duty in isolation" (*Ethics, Faith, and Reason* [Englewood Cliffs, N.J.: Prentice-Hall, 1985], pp. 83-84). God makes sense of moral obligation because his commands constitute for us our moral duties. According to Taylor, without God we literally have no moral obligations; there is no right or wrong. The atheistic moral realist rightly finds this abhorrent, but as Taylor clearly sees, on an atheistic view there simply is no ground for duty, even if moral values somehow exist.

**QUESTION 7.** We know objective moral values exist because we clearly apprehend some of them. The best way to show this is simply to describe moral situations in which we clearly see right and wrong: torturing a child, incest, rape, ethnic cleansing, racism, witch burning, the Inquisition and so forth. If someone really fails to see the objective moral truth about such matters, then he is simply morally handicapped, like a color-blind person who cannot tell the difference between red and green, and there's no reason to think that his impairment should make us call into question what we see clearly.

**QUESTION 8.** Ravi Zacharias comments, "Not one proponent of evolutionary ethics has explained how an impersonal, amoral first cause through a nonmoral process has produced a moral basis of life, while at the same time denying any objective moral basis for good and evil. Does it not seem odd that of all the permutations and combinations that a random universe might afford we should end up with the notions of the true, the good and the beautiful? In reality, why call anything good and evil? Why not call them orange and purple? That way, we settle it as different preferences? By the way, Bertrand Russell tried that latter approach and looked quite pathetic at it. . . .

"The skeptic started by presenting a long list of horrific things, saying, 'These are immoral; therefore, there is no God.' But to raise these issues as moral issues is to assume a state of affairs that evolution cannot afford. There is just no way to arrive at a morally compelling ought given the assumptions of naturalism. What then does the skeptic do? He denies objective moral values because to accept such a reality would be to allow for the possibility of God's existence. He concludes then that there really isn't such a thing as evil after all.

"This is supposed to be an answer? If DNA neither knows nor cares, what is it that prompts *our* knowing and *our* caring? . . .

"I put this theory to the test with some students at Oxford University. I asked a group of skeptics if I took a baby and sliced it to pieces before them, would I have done anything wrong? They had just denied that objective moral values exist. At my question, there was silence, and then, the lead voice in the group said, 'I would not like it, but no, I could not say you have done anything wrong.' My! What an aesthete. He would not like it. My! What irrationality—he could not brand it wrong. I only had to ask him that if evil is denied, what then remains of the original question?" (Zacharias, *Jesus Among Other Gods,* pp. 113-15).

## STUDY 4

# Can Naturalism Make Sense of the Universe?

PSALM 104:1-18, 24-32

*Purpose:* **To show that naturalism is unable to account for human consciousness and the universe's order and beauty.**

**QUESTIONS 1-2.** The psalmist personifies God as being clothed not only with certain attributes ("splendor and majesty") but with the universe itself, which shows forth his glory. Bible scholar Derek Kidner comments on verses 1-4, "These verses magnificently convey the intimate yet regal relationship of God to His world. He is distinct from His universe (whereas pantheism would have merged him with it), but He is anything but remote from it, as though He had merely set it going or given it orders. The metaphor of His taking up its parts and powers as His robe, tent, palace and chariot invites us to see the world as something He delights in, which is charged with His energy and alive with His presence. The nature miracles of Christ show that this is no fantasy" (Derek Kidner, *Psalms 73-150,* Tyndale Old Testament Commentaries [Downers Grove, Ill.: InterVarsity Press, 1973], pp. 368-69).

**QUESTION 5.** Here is a definition of naturalism by Kai Nielsen, who shares Flew's objection to theism: "Naturalism denies that there are any spiritual or supernatural realities. There are, that is, no purely mental substances and there are no supernatural realities transcendent to the world or at least we have no good ground for believing that there are such realities or perhaps even for believing that there could be such realities. It is the view that anything that exists is ultimately composed of physical components" (Kai Nielsen, "Naturalistic Explanations of Theistic Belief," in *A Companion to Philosophy of Religion,* ed. P. Quinn and C. Taliaferro [Oxford: Blackwell, 1997], p. 402).

**QUESTION 6.** Philosopher John Frame responds to Flew's parable with one of his own.

Once upon a time, two explorers came upon a clearing in the jungle. A man was there, pulling weeds, applying fertilizer, trimming branches. The man turned to the explorers and introduced himself as the royal gardener. One explorer shook his hand and exchanged pleasantries. The other ignored the gardener and turned away.

"There can be no gardener in this part of the jungle," he said. "This must be some trick. Someone is trying to discredit our secret findings."

They pitched camp. And every day the gardener arrived to tend the garden. Soon it was bursting with perfectly arranged blooms.

But the skeptical explorer insisted, "He's only doing it because we are here—to fool us into thinking that this is a royal garden."

One day the gardener took them to the royal palace and introduced the explorers to a score of officials who verified the gardener's status. Then the skeptic tried a last resort, "Our senses are deceiving us. There is no gardener, no blooms, no palace, no officials. It's all a hoax!"

Finally the believing explorer despaired, "But what remains of your original assertion? Just how does this mirage differ from a real gardener?" (Quoted in Zacharias, *Jesus Among Other Gods,* p. 167; see also John Frame, "God and Biblical Language: Transcendence and Immanence" in *God's Inerrant Word,* ed. J. W. Montgomery [Minneapolis: Bethany Fellowship, 1974], p. 171)

**QUESTIONS 7-8.** The psalmist associates wisdom (v. 24) and joy (v. 31) with God's many creative works, thus communicating that God took delight and gave thought to all that he created. This psalm envisions creation's awe of God in poetic language—he looks at the earth, and it trembles—and elsewhere in Scripture we read of creation singing praise to God and awaiting his restoration. See, for example, Jesus' words in Luke 19:40 (cf. Hab 2:11) and the apostle Paul's in Romans 8:19-22 and Romans 1:20.

**QUESTION 9.** "How is it possible for conscious states to depend upon brain states?" asks materialist philosopher Colin McGinn. "How can technicolour phenomenology arise from soggy grey matter? . . . How could the aggregation of millions of individually insentient neurons generate subjective awareness? We know that brains are the *de facto* causal basis of consciousness, but we have, it seems, no understanding of how this can be so. It strikes us as miraculous, eerie, even faintly comic" (*The Problem of Consciousness* [Oxford: Basil Blackwell, 1990], p. 1).

Another prominent philosopher, Ned Block, agrees: "We have no conception of our physical or functional nature that allows us to understand how it could explain our subjective experience . . . [i]n the case of consciousness we have nothing—zilch—worthy of being called a research program, nor are there any substantive proposals about starting one. . . . Researchers are stumped" (Block in *A Companion to the Philosophy of Mind*, ed. Samuel Guttenplan [Malden, Mass.: Blackwell, 1994], p. 211).

**QUESTION 10.** Christian philosopher Gary Habermas has debated the renowned atheist Antony Flew for over twenty years, developing a friendship in the process. The philosophy journal *Philosophia Christi* reports that after their dialogue on the resurrection, "Flew explained to Habermas that he was considering becoming a theist. While Flew did not change his position at that time, he concluded that certain philosophical and scientific considerations were causing him to do some serious rethinking. He characterized his position as that of atheism standing in tension with several huge question marks. Then, a year later, in January 2004, Flew informed Habermas that he had indeed become a theist. While still rejecting the concept of special revelation, whether Christian, Jewish or Islamic, nonetheless he had concluded that theism was true. In Flew's words, he simply 'had to go where the evidence leads' " (Gary Habermas's interview with Antony Flew, "My Pilgrimage from Atheism to Theism," *Philosophia Christi* [winter 2005], also available online at <www.biola.edu/antonyflew/index.cfm>).

## STUDY 5
# Is God Knowable?
PSALM 34:4-10; HEBREWS 11:1-3, 6

*Purpose:* **To show that God is knowable and that a foundational belief in him is reasonable.**

**QUESTION 1.** Regarding *radiant* in verse 4, Derek Kidner comments, "Radiant is a word found again in Isaiah 60:5, where it describes a mother's face lighting up at the sight of her children, long given up for lost. Using other terms, Exodus 34:29 tells of Moses' face shining as he came down from the mountain, and 2 Corinthians 3:18 relates this to a Christian's growing likeness to his Lord. In other words, radiance is delight but also glory; a transformation of the whole person" (Derek Kidner, *Psalms 1-72*, Tyndale Old Testament Commentaries [Downers Grove, Ill.: InterVarsity Press, 1973], p. 139).

**QUESTION 2.** David goes on to define what fearing God means in verses 11-14, and Proverbs 9:10 says, "The fear of the Lord is the beginning of wisdom, and knowledge of the Holy One is understanding." The biblical writers often characterize such fear not only as a holy reverence but also in relational terms; that is, entrusting and surrendering our lives to God with a confident hope in his unfailing love and provision (as depicted in vv. 4-10; see also Ps 128:1-4; 145:18-19; 147:11).

**QUESTION 3.** In his book *God in the Dark: The Assurance of Faith Beyond a Shadow of a Doubt*, Os Guinness writes, "Think back to some crisis. . . . What did your attitudes then show you of your real view of God? Or think back over some deep personal concern and the way it was brought to prayer. In situations like these we see our real views of God. *What faith is asking always reveals what it is assuming*" ([Wheaton, Ill.: Crossway, 1996], p. 70, emphasis added). Guinness describes the struggling person in a chapter aptly titled "Faith out of Focus": "For some reason or other a believer gets into his head such a wrong idea of God that it comes between him and God or between him and trusting God. Since he does not recognize what he is doing, he blames God rather than his faulty picture, little realizing that God is not like that at all. Unable to see God as he is, he cannot trust him as he should, and doubt is the result. . . . *If our picture of God is wrong, then our whole presupposition of what it is possible for God to be or do is correspondingly altered*" (*God in the Dark*, pp. 67, 69, emphasis added).

**QUESTION 5.** Someone might object that an atheist or an adherent to some nonpersonal religious faith like Taoism could also claim to know their beliefs in a properly basic way. Certainly, they could *claim* such a thing; but what does that prove? Imagine that you were locked in a room with four color-blind people, all of whom claimed that there is no difference between red and green. Suppose you tried to convince them by showing them colored pictures of red and green objects and asking, "Can't you *see* the difference?" Of course, they would see no difference at all and would dismiss your claim to see different colors as delusory. In terms of *showing* who's right, there would be a complete standoff. But would their denial of the difference between red and green or your inability to show them that you are right do anything logically either to render your belief false or to invalidate your experience? Obviously not! In the same way the person who has actually come to know God as a living reality in his life can know with assurance that his experience is no delusion, regardless of what the atheist or Taoist tells him.

   In a recent discussion, philosopher William Alston points out that in such a situation neither party knows how to demonstrate to the other that he alone has a veridical (true), rather than delusory, experience. But this stand-off does not undermine the rationality of belief in God, for *even if the believer's process of forming his belief were as reliable as can be,* he'd still have no way of giving a noncircular proof of this fact. Thus, the believer's inability to provide such a proof does not nullify the rationality of his belief. Still it remains the case that in such a situation, although the believer may *know* that his belief is true, both parties are at a complete loss to *show* the truth of their respective beliefs to the other party. How is one to break this deadlock? Alston answers that the believer should do whatever is feasible to find common ground, like logic and empirical facts, by means of which he can show in a noncircular way whose view is correct. See William Alston, "Religious Diversity and Perceptual Knowledge of God," *Faith and Philosophy* 5 [1988]: 433-48).

**QUESTIONS 9-10.** The Scriptures contend that our knowledge of God, others and even our world is *relational*. We do not know mere propositions "out there"—for example, "God exists"—for to know this truth necessarily implies some sort of relationship with the subject. We are persons in relation to other persons, and we know subjects in relation to other subjects. Christian philosopher Esther Lightcap Meek explains, "Knowing involves statements, but it doesn't mistakenly divorce those statements from the knower who is affirming them. . . . Knowing is, at its heart, an act. To act is to live, embody, knowledge. The act of knowing is a profoundly human one. And it is a struggle toward coherence" (Meek, *Longing to Know: The Philosophy of Knowledge for Ordinary People* [Grand Rapids: Brazos Press, 2003], pp. 57, 73).

John Calvin writes in the opening chapter of his *Institutes,* "Our wisdom, in so far as it ought to be deemed true and solid Wisdom, consists almost entirely of two parts: the knowledge of God and of ourselves." He argues that we know only as we know God, and we come to know God as we in turn gain knowledge of ourselves through his Word and the work of his Holy Spirit in us. Such knowledge is relational and reciprocal.

**QUESTION 11.** The Hebrew word for "to know" (*yada*) found in the Old Testament connotes a very personal knowledge of something or someone and is often used to describe the marital intimacy of a husband and wife as well as God's relationship with his people.

## STUDY 6

# What Difference Does God Make?

JOHN 1:1-18

*Purpose:* **To show that God has made himself known uniquely through Jesus Christ.**

**QUESTIONS 1-2.** With the opening phrase "in the beginning," John opens his story of Jesus not with his earthly birth, but remarkably, Jesus' presence at the birth of creation. He identifies Jesus as "the Word," the Word who "was with God," and even more, "the Word [who] was God." Thus right away John affirms Jesus' deity: He is no mere teacher or miracle worker, but God in the flesh. he further supports this statement by attesting to Jesus' role in creation, noting that "without him nothing was made that has been made" (v. 3).

In identifying Jesus as "the Word," John follows in the line of Old Testament prophets who proclaimed and esteemed the words God spoke to them and through them. God revealed himself through his spoken word and now, through his incarnate Word. Just as God spoke in Genesis 1 and the world came into being, so he sends his Word into the world in the birth of Jesus. Bible scholar Rodney Whitacre comments, "In the beginning the Word already *was*. So we actually start before the beginning, outside of time and space in eternity. If we want to understand who Jesus is, John says, we must begin with the relationship shared between the Father and the Son 'before the world began' (Jn. 17:5; 24). This relationship is the central revelation of this Gospel and the key to understanding all that Jesus says and does" (Rodney A. Whitacre, *John*, The IVP New Testament Commentary Series [Downers Grove, Ill.: InterVarsity Press, 1999], p. 50).

**QUESTION 3.** The word *light* appears twenty-four times in John's Gospel and seven times in this opening passage alone. John sees light as one of the themes of Jesus' ministry, and Jesus uses the word in relation to himself and his mission. For instance, Jesus says, "Put your trust in the light while you have it, so that you may become sons of light" (Jn 12:36). Echoing John 1:4-9, Jesus declares, "I am the light of the world. Whoever follows me will never walk in darkness, but will have the light of life" (Jn 8:12; see also Jn 9:5).

Similarly, John uses *life* thirty-six times in his Gospel. John records many instances when Jesus uses the word in relation to himself and his Heavenly Father. See for example, Jesus' many references to "eternal life" with God, including John 3:15, 16, 36; 4:14, 36. Jesus announces that he is "the bread of life" in John 6:35 and that "he who comes to me will never go hungry, and he who believes in me will never be thirsty."

**QUESTION 4.** Regarding verses 14-18, Rodney Whitacre writes, "We now come to the climax of the prologue. There have been many references to the incarnation in the previous verses, but they were expressed in a veiled way. In fact, everything up to this point could even be interpreted in a way that would have been compatible, even attractive, to various ancient thinkers. But now comes the break with all non-Christian thought. This Word, the agent of creation, has become a creature. He who brought the universe into existence is newborn within the universe as a human being. This thought is so familiar in Christianity we may no longer be staggered by it" (*John*, p. 58).

**QUESTION 5.** The mystery of the incarnation, and hence the Trinity, has sometimes been misunderstood as a contradiction, for how can God be both human and divine? Christian philosopher Norman Geisler responds, "How can God be three and yet one? Isn't this a contradiction? It would seem that God could be one and not three, or three and not one. But He cannot be both three and one at the same time. It would be a violation of the most fundamental law of thought, the law of noncontradiction.

"First of all, the Christian belief in a Trinity of three persons in one God is not a contradiction. A contradiction occurs only when something is both A and non-A at the same time and in the same sense. God is both three and one at the same time but not *in the same sense*. He is three in persons but one in essence. He is three persons but only one in nature.

"It would be a contradiction to say that God had three natures in one nature or three persons in one person. But it is not a contradiction to claim God has three persons in one nature. God is like a triangle. Each corner is not the same as the whole triangle. Or, God is like one to the third power ($1^3$). $1 \times 1 \times 1 = 1$. God is not $1 + 1 + 1 = 3$, which is tritheism or polytheism. God is one God, manifested eternally and simultaneously in three distinct persons.

"God is love (1 John 4:16). But to have love, there must be a lover (Father), a loved one (Son), and a spirit of love (Holy Spirit). So, love itself is a tri-unity.

"Another illustration of the Trinity is that God is like my mind, ideas, and words. There is a unity between them, yet they are distinct from each other.

"Of course, the Trinity is a mystery. It goes beyond reason without going against reason. We can apprehend it, but we cannot completely comprehend it" (Geisler, "Who Made God?" pp. 29-30).

**QUESTIONS 6, 9.** Regarding the uniqueness of Jesus' incarnation and crucifixion, Ravi Zacharias observes, "The cross uniquely reveals not a God who is taciturn and disengaged from the human scene, but a God who is right in the middle of our conflicts and struggles. This is not the Buddhist notion of retreating from the real world through monastic self-renunciation or of counteracting with good to offset the ever-present evil. This is not the Hindu notion of a pantheon of gods whose life so transcends this earthly domain as to be wedded to myth inextricably. Nor is this the Islamic concept that endeavors to build an earthly kingdom by whatever means it takes, even the sword. *This is the very incarnation, the embodiment of the Everlasting One*, to communicate to a world that hungers for relational bliss and that yearns for a love so supreme that all else may be expelled—and yet a world which convulses with fractured kinships. . . .

"When man lives apart from God, chaos is the norm. When man lives with God, as revealed in the incarnation of Jesus Christ, the hungers of the mind and heart find their fulfillment. For in Christ we find coherence and consolation as He reveals to us, in the most verifiable terms of truth and experience, the nature of man, the nature of reality, the nature of history, the nature of our destiny, and the nature of suffering" (Ravi Zacharias, *Can Man Live Without God?* [Dallas: Word, 1994], pp. 176, 178-79).

**QUESTIONS 10-11.** Jesus underscores that knowledge of him involves an intimate relationship; in the parable of the ten virgins he is the bridegroom coming for his bride (see Mt 25:1-13; cf. 9:15). Five virgins were wise, yet five were foolish because their awareness of the bridegroom's return did not move them to act upon this knowledge until it was too late. They are shut out of the wedding feast. Significantly, Jesus' response through the bridegroom's voice is almost identical to his remarks in Matthew 7:23: "I tell you the truth, *I don't know you*" (Mt 25:12, emphasis added).

The conclusion that God exists is but the first step of our journey, albeit a crucial one. The Bible says, "He who would come to God must believe that he exists and that he is a rewarder of those who seek him" (Heb 11:6). If we have come to believe that he exists, we must now seek him in the confidence that if we do so with our whole heart, he will reward us with the personal knowledge of himself.